How Intelligent Men Find Love Offline

Meet Women Without Apps

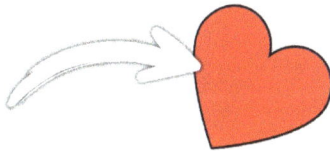

Eddy Baller

Dedication

Dedicated to my wife, who experienced the principles in this book firsthand—
though from the other side—when we met one rainy day on a downtown street.
Since then, she's been by my side through every challenge and triumph, supporting
me all the way to the success of this business today.

For one-on-one men's dating coaching reach out to me at eddy@conquerandwin.com

Coaching is available online and in person, in your city, anywhere on planet earth.

Table of Contents

INTRODUCTION

You're about to change your love life in ways you never imagined possible

You may worry your looks, money, status, height, or even race aren't good enough to attract great women.

Or maybe you do get dates, but not with women you're excited about. Or you go on a date that seems good—then she's suddenly "too busy."

Some of you may even end up in relationships, but not with the kind of women you truly want. Some turn out toxic.

Whether it's getting dates, keeping them, or attracting the right women, this book will change your love life.

I'll help you grow the confidence and communication skills to naturally attract beautiful women—without apps, bars, or clubs.

The truth is, most men today have become dependent on apps.

Dating has turned into a weird online shopping cart where you scroll through a menu, and add "items" to your shopping cart—except this shopping cart rejects you 99% of the time.

It's an unnatural way to meet women, and it leaves most men frustrated, burned out, and doubting themselves.

This book shows you how to meet women in the real world again, the old fashioned way, by talking to them.

It's built on 26 years of experience, including 14 years of coaching men, which gave me deeper insight into dating psychology and what actually works in real life.

Men have been lied to. Movies, "experts," and even well-meaning family all give terrible advice. Being "nice" isn't enough—it just leads to years of frustration.

I lived that frustration. I was the "great friend" to too many women. Then I learned the truth: dating doesn't work the way we've been told.

It's time for your awakening. Your new start. Get ready for your adventure.

MY STORY

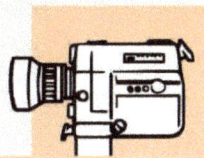

> I started my "dating career" as a tall, skinny guy with bad acne, depression and social anxiety. Not the best resume for attracting women...

In my late teens and early twenties, I was a tall, lanky guy with social anxiety, depression, bad health, and painful acne that left scars.

Sure, I was tall (as many shorter guys loved to remind me), but looking like a toothpick didn't make me feel confident.

I avoided meeting strangers whenever possible, and if more than one person was around, I'd break into a sweat.

Not exactly the qualities that attract women.

I tried for years to put on muscle—lifting weights, reading fitness magazines, chugging weight gainers—but nothing worked.

For my skin, I took antibiotics for years, which barely touched the acne and probably damaged my health. The acne fueled my depression, and even when it cleared, the depression stuck around.

Eventually, I started experimenting with different ways to meet women and ended up in a relationship with someone I met through a friend.

It turned out to be toxic. She had a volatile personality—happy one moment, furious the next. Later I realized it was just manipulation. By flipping her moods, she could get me to do anything. Eventually, I wised up and left her.

"NO WOMAN WAKES UP SAYING, 'GOD, I HOPE I DON'T GET SWEPT OFF MY FEET TODAY!"

— HITCH

MY STORY

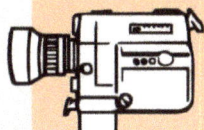

But I hadn't learned my lesson yet. Years later, I got into another relationship with a woman who acted the same way. I stayed for almost a year, putting up with constant emotional abuse.

After two toxic relationships, I made a decision: never again. I was going to meet the kind of women I actually wanted. Over time, my social anxiety, depression, and health problems began to fade.

Around then, my dad suggested online dating. I gave it a shot—and eventually figured out how to make it work.

> **Online dating is just online marketing. It takes the "balls" out of the equation. Meeting women in real life requires courage and social skills.**

Even though I felt good about how I was doing online, most dates didn't turn into second dates or anything physical.

One day I realized I wasn't the Casanova I thought I was. **At a crosswalk, a beautiful blonde was standing right beside me, and I couldn't say a word.** That's when it hit me: online dating had given me a false sense of confidence. **Behind a screen I could type messages, but face-to-face I froze.**

I started brainstorming how to crack the code. While searching online, I came across a video of a guy approaching two women at a café patio. All he did was compliment them. I thought, that's it? That's all you have to do? It blew my mind.

Of course, it wasn't actually that easy—especially for someone socially awkward like me. You can't just walk up and blurt out a compliment. Women don't respond well to that. There's more to the equation, but at least I had stumbled onto a piece of the puzzle.

After months of trial, error, and frustration, I decided to get help. **I found a coach and signed up for a bootcamp. That decision changed everything.**

MY STORY

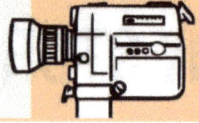

In two hours I met more women than I had in 3 to 4 months on my own.

I took what I learned in that bootcamp and kept going out every day to talk to women. Over the years I discovered things most guys couldn't imagine.

Learning how to meet women offline was one of the best decisions I ever made.

Men are told to be passive or "nice," but that advice works against us—and against women too. **Most guys are literally doing the opposite of what attracts women.** (More on that later in the book.)

I started teaching other men because I wanted to push myself further. Teaching forces you to learn at a deeper level than just practicing alone.

After years of "practice," **I built up experience approaching countless thousands of women and going on more than a thousand dates.**

Then one day while coaching a student, **I met the woman who eventually became my wife—using the exact same approach I'll be teaching you here.**

I launched this business in 2011 out of passion, and it grew into my career and lifestyle. You never know where a single conversation might lead.

MOTIVATION ONLY GETS YOU STARTED.
COMMITMENT IS WHAT GETS YOU TO THE
FINISH LINE.

HOW TO GET SUCCESS WITH THIS BOOK

NOTE: Some sections may not apply to you. If you're not insecure about your appearance, and you're already happy with your fitness or other areas of life, skip ahead to the challenges where you'll learn how to start conversations with women —offline.

Here are some pointers to make this book work for you: **it won't work if you don't. If you skip the exercises and avoid talking to real women, nothing will change.**

Start adjusting your daily habits and notice how you think. Don't just read this passively—use it. Write in the notepaper, fill out the journal, and complete every exercise.

A daily journal is essential. It keeps you accountable and shows what you're doing right or wrong.

You'll know if you went out every day or just once or twice a week. Without records, it's easy to fool yourself into thinking you're doing more than you are.

Later, looking back at your journal will be proof of your progress.

So before you read further, make a commitment. Commit to doing the exercises, writing down your results, and staying consistent until you get what you came for.

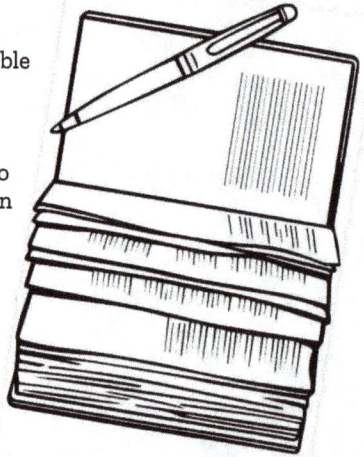

Sign your declaration below.

I _____name_____ commit to doing my best, every day, and will follow through on all exercises, and keep working on things until I get what I came here to learn:

SIGNATURE: **DATE:**

HOW TO GET SUCCESS WITH THIS BOOK

If a challenge feels easy, do it anyway. Many guys say something is "easy" even when they've never actually done it. Follow through, and if it really is easy, move on to the next challenge. But don't drop the easy ones—keep them as part of the daily social habits you're building.

Get out and practice daily: Consistency is the only way to get good at this.

Don't get down on yourself. You'll hit bumps, face rejection, and go through some lows. But if you stick with it, you'll improve and meet great women for both dates and relationships.

Re-read each section of the book. You can't just skim it once and expect it to stick. It takes repetition to fully absorb the lessons.

The Power of Habit

Your habits make life easier by letting your mind go on autopilot and complete tasks automatically. That's useful—until bad habits take over. Then failure just repeats itself on autopilot.

When you feel too lazy to try something new, it's usually your habits pulling you back. It's always easier to stick with the same routine—the path of least resistance —especially when the new behavior feels difficult.

That's why starting a new routine, and sticking with it, can feel so hard.

HOW TO GET SUCCESS WITH THIS BOOK

Your whole life, you've had the habit of not talking to beautiful women you see offline. That habit has been reinforced by fear—fear of approaching, fear of rejection, fear of not being good enough.

Now you're on a new journey to create the love life you want, and that requires new habits.

To succeed, you'll need to break the old ones and push past the fear of approaching attractive women. This is especially true if you struggle with self-esteem or feel you're not attractive enough.

FEAR NOT

The anxieties we feel are not correct by default, even though they feel that way. Just like our thoughts are not correct just because we had them. Our feelings and mindsets will change over time by taking the right actions.

To create new habits you must:

- ✅ Practice daily.
- ✅ Challenge habitual thoughts.
- ✅ Correct negative behaviors.
- ✅ Build an environment or lifestyle that supports the habit.
- ✅ Remove distractions.
- ✅ Set clear goals.
- ✅ Hold yourself accountable.
- ✅ Schedule your new habit.

New Habits I will Start (examples):

- ☐ Gym
- ☐ Running
- ☐ Healthy eating
- ☐ Making eye contact
- ☐ Starting conversations with women
- ☐ Asking them on dates

Others? Make a note below.

_____

_____

_____

HOW TO GET SUCCESS WITH THIS BOOK

Now choose one habit from your list and pick a date to start working on it.

I will start _____ **on (Date):** _____

◆ Create a Lifestyle

The point of this book is to help you build a lifestyle where you naturally meet and attract the kind of women you want—without swiping through apps or treating dating like online shopping.

◆ Seek Rejection

We usually avoid anything that causes pain—and most of the time that makes sense. But our bigger goals often demand uncomfortable, even painful experiences to get what we want.

"Growing pains" are part of learning. At first you'll feel lost and frustrated, but with experience you'll find your way.

When it comes to getting good with women, the only path is through rejection.

There are no shortcuts.

This process, for those who stick to it, will make you tougher and more emotionally resilient.

By doing this you will become one of very few men to ever meet women in this way.

You'll stand out among the crowd and learn new skills other guys will never get a handle on, and get your ideal relationship doing it.

HOW TO GET SUCCESS WITH THIS BOOK

◆ Remove Distractions & Negativity

As exciting as it is to meet new women, it can also be emotionally draining.

If your mind is overloaded with negative news, endless Instagram scrolling, constant notifications, and general anxiety from all that noise, your results will suffer.

Think about it: learning something this emotionally challenging requires all the support you can get—especially from your own inner dialogue. What you tell yourself matters.

When you absorb negativity from the outside world, your inner voice will echo it back. Your entire outlook—on life and on yourself—gets shaped by those ideas.

And if you already feel lousy because of bad news, how motivated do you think you'll be to push yourself into a high-anxiety situation like approaching an attractive woman?

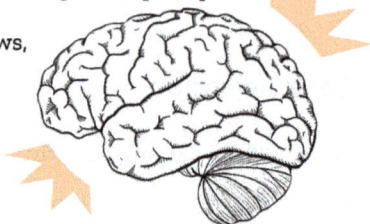

> **Give yourself the emotional support you need to become successful with women by eliminating DISTRACTIONS.**

Some distractions include:

✗ News
✗ Social media
✗ Negative friends or family
✗ "Influencers"

HOW TO GET SUCCESS WITH THIS BOOK

Make a commitment to cut out distractions that interfere with your goals.

When I wrote this book, I went on a "news fast." I removed my Google news feed, deleted Facebook and Instagram, and instantly freed up mental space.

These distractions weren't just wasting time—they were planting ideas in my head that kept recycling throughout the day. Now, if I want information, I look it up directly instead of being fed an endless stream of junk.

Even after the first day, my mind felt clearer and it was easier to focus.

In the past, I followed tons of YouTube channels about social and cultural problems. At first it felt informative, but eventually my head was filled with negativity and anger. I went from positive to bitter. The solution was simple: I unfollowed them.

Not long after, I returned to being positive and productive.

What are you going to eliminate or reduce to remove bad influences?

- ☐ Instagram
- ☐ Facebook
- ☐ Notices on my phone
- ☐ News feeds
- ☐ Emails newsletters
- ☐ A negative friend
- ☐ A bad habit
- ☐ Reddit Forums
- ☐ TV
- ☐ Desktop notices
- ☐ Influencers

Which negative influences will you eliminate? Make notes below.

_____

_____

CONFIDENCE VS. LOOKS

Looks matter, but not as much as you might think

Are you worried about your looks? If not, skip this section. But if you think beautiful women won't give you a chance because of your looks, keep reading.

Here's the truth: **looks matter much less offline**. In the real world, confidence, presence, and how you carry yourself play a far bigger role.

But online? If you're not good-looking, it's a massive disadvantage. **Apps are designed like shopping carts**—you're a product on a shelf, and **women swipe past 99% of the options.**

Many guys are worried about being short, overweight, ugly, "the wrong ethnicity" or even having average looks.

One problem, besides self-esteem, is misunderstanding how women find men attractive. **As men, we judge women by their looks.**

Women do not find men attractive the same way we find them attractive. We are not the same and are not looking for the same qualities.

And it's not that looks don't matter at all because **looks do have an effect**. But to a much lesser degree than most men think. Your confidence plays a bigger role here.

> ### Men and women are not the same, and we're not attracted to each other in the same ways.

Good looks are just a (helpful) bonus for men. You could be a butt ugly man who oozes confidence and gets the most attractive women. Or you could be an attractive man who is shy and keeps to himself, and be alone on the weekend.

I've seen this regularly after coaching men for more than a decade. I've had clients who you'd look at and think, "that guy will NEVER get an attractive woman".

LOOKS MATTER MORE TO MEN THAN THEY DO TO WOMEN. IT'S OUR OWN SELF PERCEPTION WHICH HURTS US WHEN WE FEEL NEGATIVE ABOUT OUR LOOKS. WORKING ON YOUR APPEARANCE CAN HELP BOOST YOUR SELF CONFIDENCE, AND CONFIDENCE IS THE KEY TO ATTRACTING WOMEN. IF YOU FEEL GOOD ABOUT YOURSELF THIS WILL IMPROVE YOUR RELATIONSHIPS WITH EVERYONE.

CONFIDENCE VS. LOOKS

Can a short, fat guy with no style get attractive women?

You just read the title above and probably thought, "No way." But here's an example that proves otherwise:

One of my former clients was a 40-year-old Chinese man (he's probably still Chinese)—short, pot-bellied, badly dressed, and with a heavy accent that made him hard to understand at times.

Yet with persistence, and some adjustments to his style, he started dating younger women—including a cute 22-year-old local girl.

His success shattered my own skepticism and showed me that **offline, confidence and personality matter far more than looks.**

◆ How about a man with a stutter?

Another case was an Indian student of mine in his early thirties. Not bad looking, but nerdy, with a stutter that got worse when he was nervous—especially around beautiful women.

He faced plenty of frustration, but he stuck with the program. Then one day he texted me with incredible news: he had met a beautiful woman while walking down the street (the same way you'll learn in this book). After a short conversation, he invited her for coffee, and they sat down to chat.

(Continues at the arrow on the next page)

> ### Bold, assertive men will attract more women than men with good looks alone.

CONFIDENCE VS. LOOKS

After an hour he made a bold move: **he invited her home.**

What happened? **She said yes.**

They got to his place and she kept repeating, "I can't believe I'm doing this!" He just smiled.

Long story short, she spent the night. They ended up seeing each other a few more times before she had to leave the city because she was moving.

This isn't some model-good looking stud we're talking about.

He's an average, nerdy guy who has a speech impediment, an Indian accent, and no prior experience with women.

He still made magic happen, and so can you.

CONFIDENCE VS. LOOKS

◆ How about status or money?

This is another example of how looks don't matter. Now you're probably thinking, "I knew it, it's all about money!". Not exactly.

You'll never see men dating ugly women for status or money.

That doesn't matter to us as men.

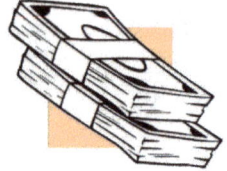

We're judging women for physical attraction, period.

So what are women really attracted to? At the core, **women want balls.** They're drawn to bold, confident men who speak their minds and don't crumble under pressure.

Status ties into this because it projects the same qualities as confidence. Men with status usually had to earn it—and that path required boldness, assertiveness, and resilience. That's why status signals a man's ability to protect and provide, at least on the surface.

Times may have changed, but human attraction hasn't. Assertiveness is still magnetic, and status often comes packaged with it.

Even if you don't have status, money, or model looks, you can develop confidence and assertiveness.

That alone makes you stand out like a man of status. And this isn't about faking it —it's about becoming that man. Which is exactly what you're starting to do now.

Create a life other people want to be a part of

A NOTE ABOUT LOOKS AND ATTRACTION

Looks do affect attraction—it's a fact. Who doesn't like good-looking people?

The problem is many men exaggerate how much looks really matter, or they use it as an excuse.

You don't need to be a model to get great women. Offline, social skills and confidence go much further than looks.

That's why it's smarter to focus on meeting women in real life. By building confidence and sharpening your social skills, you'll attract far more women than relying on appearance alone.

That said, improving your looks still helps. Small upgrades boost your confidence and how you feel about yourself. Each improvement builds on the others, creating a much stronger overall impact.

HOW TO UPGRADE YOUR APPEARANCE

Can an "ugly" or "average" man improve his looks? Hell yes—I did it myself. **If you're self-conscious about your appearance, it will drag down your confidence.** So to boost confidence in every area, it makes sense to improve your looks too.

A lot of guys who feel insecure about their appearance act the part. That usually means bad posture, poorly fitted clothes, zero style, and being out of shape. Sure, you can't change your genetics—but chances are, you haven't made the most of what you've got.

Some improvements take time, but others are as simple as visiting a clothing store or getting a fresh haircut. The next three challenges will help you upgrade your appearance, energy, health, and confidence.

Focusing only on dating skills without working on your health, fitness, and style is like fighting with one hand tied behind your back.

Looks may not be the most important factor in attraction, but they directly affect how you feel about yourself. Improve them, and your confidence will rise with them.

UPGRADE #1 A New Look

Men's style is mostly about wearing clothes that fit well. Too many guys who worry about their looks dress sloppy. Dress with the intention of looking good—don't just throw something on. Dress on purpose.

Notice how your clothes make you feel. If it's anything less than great, it's time to change things up. Only wear clothing that makes you feel attractive and confident.

HOW TO UPGRADE YOUR APPEARANCE

Upgrade #1 A New Look

It should fit your body well and not be overly baggy. Form fitting, but not tight or restrictive.

If you aren't sure what to wear, ask for somebody's opinion. Talk to an attractive girl whose opinion you trust and start learning what looks and feels good on you.

Your Challenge:

Go to a clothing store which carries well known brands. Ask an attractive female staff member, or another shopper, to give you some suggestions on where to start. Then try some items on and ask her opinion again.

This also serves the purpose of talking to an attractive woman to start building social confidence.

Do you already feel confident about what you're wearing? Complete it anyways to talk to the attractive staff member or patron. The more situations you put yourself in talking to women, the more opportunities you'll create.

BONUS CHALLENGE:

You're talking to a cute sales woman, why not ask her out? Learn a bit about her first. You'll start by asking about clothing, then bridge into something about her. You can ask something like, "So what got you working in retail?"

Go to P.51 for conversation skills

Date I will complete this Challenge:

Store I will shop at:

OUR STYLE TELLS OTHER PEOPLE
SOMETHING ABOUT WHO WE ARE.
CHOOSE WHAT YOU TELL THE WORLD.

HOW TO UPGRADE YOUR APPEARANCE

Upgrade #1 A New Look

QUESTIONS:

◆ **How did you feel trying on new clothing?**

_____

_____

_____

_____

◆ **How did it feel asking an attractive woman for her opinion on your style?**

_____

_____

_____

_____

◆ **How did the conversation go?**

_____

_____

_____

_____

◆ **Did you learn anything about her? Remember, every conversation will develop your social skills with women.**

_____

_____

_____

_____

HOW TO UPGRADE YOUR APPEARANCE

UPGRADE #2 Fitness & Health

Nobody's feels good about being overweight or underweight. "Skinny fat" isn't a great look on men, nor is the "dad bod".

Being fit is so much more than just looking good. Your energy and confidence is affected by your fitness.

The "dad bod" isn't a good look for men.

Being fit means higher confidence, better fitting clothes, and better posture. It also means being more attractive.

Starting point:

Find a personal trainer or choose one fitness coach to follow online. There are tons of trainers out there, but stick with one to get consistent advice.

Personally, I like Athlean-X for clear routines and proper lifting technique, but choose whoever you connect with.

Once you've picked your source, start working out. Keep it simple at first: do pushups every morning until you join a gym or get equipment. Add running or free squats. Just choose something and start now.

◆ Notes:

_____

_____

_____

HOW TO UPGRADE YOUR APPEARANCE

Upgrade #2 Fitness & Health

◆ ## Which exercise or routine will you start with?

_____

_____

_____

I will start my first workout on (Date here):

Part B

Processed foods: This is a simple way to improve your health. Stop or reduce anything processed, such as pasta, breads, desserts, soda etc.

I'm not a purist, I definitely like treats. But if you're trying to make a big difference in your health and fitness then cleaning up your diet is a must. For better information talk to a nutritionist.

Start by removing processed foods and sweets from your home.

Which foods have you removed from your kitchen?

_____

_____

_____

Avoid having to use willpower by removing processed foods from your kitchen. Replace sweets with fruits so you can counter sugar cravings.

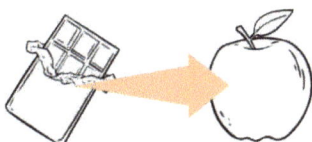

HOW TO UPGRADE YOUR APPEARANCE

UPGRADE #3 Your Posture

Your posture tells other people about your confidence levels. It's also self feedback and affects how you feel. Correct your posture to start feeling confident.

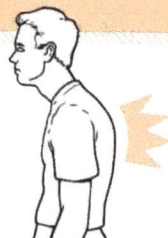

Posture has a significant effect on how other people will see you. It affects how you feel about yourself too. Bad posture looks like bad confidence. It will affect proper breathing which can make you feel anxiety.

Start doing this

Take your hands out of your pockets: Instead, let them hang by your sides and swing freely.

Keep your eyes forward and head up: Don't look at the ground. Not only does it convey a lack of confidence, but you won't have any situational awareness.

Make eye contact: Strong eye contact is key to attracting women. It shows confidence.

Stand straight: Standing straight will allow you to use your full height. Bad posture will make you shorter. It will also help proper breathing.

Exercises: Strengthen your muscles working out and by practicing good posture.

This week, starting today, I will pay attention to my posture and correct it little by little. (Self contract)

YOUR SIGNATURE HERE:

◆ One Week Checklist (Your Posture):

☐ Monday   ☐ Wednesday   ☐ Friday   ☐ Sunday

☐ Tuesday   ☐ Thursday   ☐ Saturday

HOW TO UPGRADE YOUR APPEARANCE

◆ **Change Your Inner Dialogue**

Stop telling yourself you're ugly, short, or not worthy. Phrases like "out of her league" or "girls like that don't like me" only reinforce excuses. If you keep repeating that you're unattractive, it becomes your reality.

It's normal to have features you don't like, but women aren't looking for perfection. Focus on what you can control and stop obsessing over what you can't.

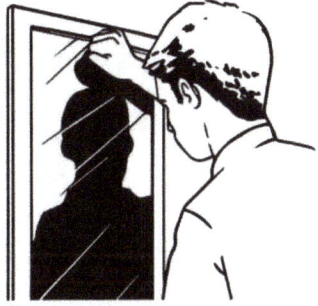

This takes work because negative thoughts are habits. To change them, redirect your attention each time your mind wanders.

Tall and skinny? Remind yourself you're built for endurance. Short and stout? Tell yourself you're built for strength.

The more you repeat these reframes, the more you'll believe them. Think of it as self-brainwashing—shaping your mind into the version you want to become.

> **Whatever you repeat to yourself on a daily basis will become your reality. Replace negative self-mantras with positive ones.**

New Mantra: Find a phrase or statement to replace, 'I'm ugly' or whichever negative mantra you're telling yourself. It can be something like, "I'm improving", "I'm working on it", "I'm ok the way I am" or whatever resonates with you.

Refocus: Steer your thoughts away from your negative thinking habits. When the thought comes up, refocus on something positive instead. It can be something you're grateful for, or the opposite side of the coin. Instead of, "I'm short and stocky" you can focus on the strength and leverage that your shape gives you.

JUST BECAUSE YOU HAVE A THOUGHT DOESN'T MAKE IT TRUE. OUR BRAINS WILL REPEAT IDEAS WE'VE COME ACROSS. YOU DON'T HAVE TO BELIEVE YOUR OWN NEGATIVE HABITUAL THINKING.

HOW TO AVOID BEING CREEPY

I get asked all the time about how to avoid being creepy. Ironically, it's usually the guys most worried about being creepy who end up acting that way. Here's why—and how to stop it.

Avoiding creepiness is easier than you think.

I like to compare it to target fixation.
If you ride a motorcycle, you know what this means.
When you're leaning left through a corner, you need to keep your eyes on where you want to go.

If instead you focus on the object you're trying to avoid, you'll steer right into it.

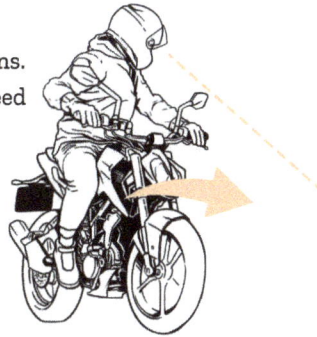

The same thing happens socially.

Many inexperienced motorcyclists crash because of target fixation. I've felt it myself—your bike follows where your eyes go. If you stare at what you want to avoid, you'll steer straight into it.

The same thing happens with guys worried about being creepy. By obsessing over it, they "steer" right into creepy behavior. Their body language turns stiff, their vibe becomes unnatural, and they start micromanaging every move instead of being themselves.

The fix is simple: **stop fixating on what you fear and focus on what you want.** Pay attention to the woman you're talking to. Be curious about her, listen, and relax. Do that, and the "creepy" vibe disappears.

When guys get self conscious, they'll often act in ways which look "creepy".

HOW TO AVOID BEING CREEPY

◆ Giving Space

Don't invade a woman's personal space. There should be a comfortable distance between the two of you. Most of the time that's about 4 to 5 feet, to start.

As a rule of thumb, if you stick your arm straight out she should be out of reach by at least a half-an-arm.

Sorry if you're used to metric...

From Seinfled: The "close talker"

◆ Pay Attention to Social Cues

Never try to force a conversation with someone who isn't interested. It'll take some time to learn the signals women give when they're uncomfortable. Some are obvious though.

Watch for these negative signals:

She's trying to walk away

She's avoiding eye contact

Crazy weather, right?! / ok
She gives you one word answers

Her body leaning away from you (you're probably too close)

She tries to keep a distance or makes more space

HOW TO AVOID BEING CREEPY

◆ **Negative signals cont'd:**

Scowling	She turns away

There are other negative signals, but these are the main ones. Keep in mind, context matters—what looks negative in one moment might not be in another, depending on the situation and the mix of signals she's giving.

Since this is a beginner's book, I won't cover every nuance. With time and experience, you'll learn to read situations better.

As for being "creepy," that often happens when guys can't read social cues. If you pay attention, you'll be fine. Don't obsess over avoiding creepiness—just relax and enjoy the conversation.

I'll cover positive body language in later chapters.

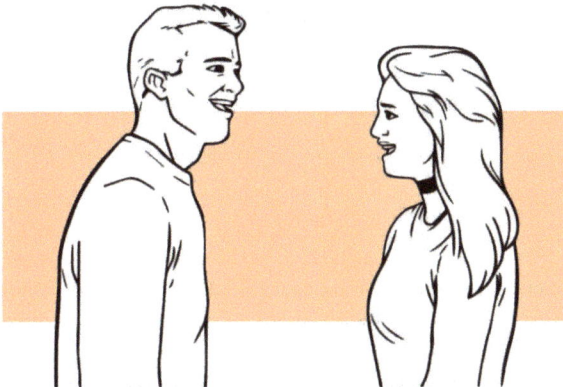

HOW TO HANDLE REJECTION

If you've ever asked out your crush and got rejected, or been told you're "just friends," you know it hurts.

Rejection will always sting, but learning how to handle it is crucial—for both your success with women and your emotional health.

If you let rejection crush you, the cost is high. You'll hesitate, hold back, and miss opportunities. Or worse, you may stop trying altogether.

> **Rejection will help make you into a stronger man IF you learn how to handle it.**

Rejection can train you to stop trying, if you don't learn to gain strength through it.

But here's the problem—you're also blocking yourself from the women who might have said yes.

By not trying, you've already rejected yourself before they even had the chance.

> **If you're not getting rejected then you're not asking out enough women.**

So what can you do to relieve some of that rejection anxiety?

◆ Steps to Deal with Social Rejection

1. Get tougher by seeking more rejection

Number one is actually to get rejected more. This is counterintuitive but you need experience getting rejected to adapt to it.

The bi-product is experience, mental toughness and dates.

AVOIDING REJECTION LIMITS YOUR OPPORTUNITIES. BY SEEKING REJECTION YOU'LL GIVE WOMEN THE CHANCE TO SAY "YES". HEARING "NO" IS PART OF THE PROCESS.

HOW TO HANDLE REJECTION

When I started amatuer boxing, punches hurt. We would spar hard and guys would get carried away.

I still remember the first real punch I took. It felt like his fist went through my brain.

Avoiding your fears will make them grow

After a while, the pain started to fade. My sensitivity to taking hits dropped—I didn't feel "soft" anymore. I could take punches and keep moving. Before, every hit stunned me and I needed time to recover.

Rejection works the same way. The more "punches" you take, the less they affect you. (And don't worry—nobody's actually going to punch you!)

The bigger danger isn't rejection—it's avoiding it. Every time you avoid rejection, your fear grows stronger.

This is the basis of exposure therapy. Therapists help patients by exposing them to their fears, a little at a time.

Do the same for yourself: improve at your own pace, but always push the envelope. Face your fears directly, and eventually the sting will fade away.

2. **Breathing to calm your rejection anxiety**

If you ask someone out and get rejected, focus on your breathing. We start breathing shallowly when we're stressed. That makes anxiety worse.

HOW TO HANDLE REJECTION

Take control of your breath to interrupt this pattern. Take deep breaths and exhale slowly. This will help to calm the nerves so that you can clear your mind and move past it.

Use breath control before going into situations which cause anxiety, too.

1. DEEP BREATH   **2. NOW EXHALE SLOWLY** for 5 seconds   **3. REPEAT**

3. Mindset

Rejection is often blown out of proportion. Instead, look at the positives. **Getting rejected means you actually asked her out instead of just imagining it.** Think about how many other guys wanted to but never tried.

By taking action, you've already set yourself apart. Now you can move on to the next opportunity—because there are countless women out there you haven't even met yet.

4. Body Language

One common mistake I see after rejection is guys shoving their hands in their pockets and staring at the ground.

That body language screams defeat—and acting defeated only makes you feel worse.

HOW TO HANDLE REJECTION

4. **Body Language /** After a rejection, do this Instead:

Lift your head up   Look straight ahead   Keep your hands out of your pockets

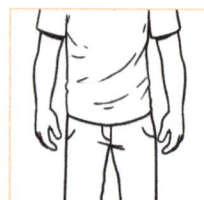

Walk away tall, with your shoulders back and chest out, like a confident man

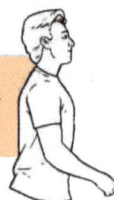

5. **Don't React**

Act like nothing happened. When you walk away after rejection as if it's no big deal, you're showing emotional control. Never turn it into a drama.

By staying non-reactive, you send a powerful signal to your brain that this is just a non-event. No big deal—you're moving on, and your emotions will follow.

No!

Act like the man you want to be to develop emotional control.

HOW TO HANDLE REJECTION

6. Don't Put Women on a Pedestal

Putting women on a pedestal decreases your own self worth. This makes rejection feel worse. I will cover this in more detail later on.

7. Move on

When a girl rejects you, it's time to move on. She's probably not as great as you think.
Maybe she seems great because she's beautiful. That's just lust.

Our thinking gets clouded by lust. We project ideas about women being angels, perfect beings, infallible etc just because our balls are calling the shots.

MOVE ON

You deserve better than to be fixated on one woman who's not interested.

DON'T PUT WOMEN ON A PEDESTAL

A lot of guys don't realize they're putting women on a pedestal. This repels attractive women because they get it all of the time from "nice guys".

If you say things like:

- "She's out of my league"
- "She'd never go for a guy like me"
- "She's not like 'that' "
- "She's an angel"

Then you're putting women on a pedestal. This will usually result in low confidence behaviors.

Examples of low confidence behaviors:

✗ Not setting boundaries and tolerating bad behavior (she can do anything she wants, and you just take it)

✗ Paying for everything (she doesn't reciprocate)

✗ Driving her around on errands and fixing her problems.

✗ Not asking her out (romantically)

✗ Asking her out but acting timid and uncertain "Um, maybe if you want to, we can go out sometime? I mean, if you're ever free..."

And many more. Usually, you're the one doing all the work, chasing her or paying out of your pocket.

This kind of thinking will prevent you from dating the kind of women you want. And the women you don't want will take advantage of you.

One of the problems with guys putting women on a pedestal is they assume they're little angels or "pure" in some way.

Putting women on a pedestal will limit your options for quality relationships.

DON'T PUT WOMEN ON A PEDESTAL

Women aren't innocent angels just because they're attractive. They have the same flaws and weaknesses men do. A beautiful woman can have just as many bad habits and poor relationship skills as anyone else.

The moment you stop putting women on a pedestal, you'll open up your options. Take the time to actually get to know her before deciding how amazing she really is.

> **Toxic women will take advantage of men who don't set boundaries.**

Your Value as a Man:

Don't base your worth as a man on what women think of you.

If you do, you'll ride an emotional roller coaster—feeling high when a woman likes you and crashing when one doesn't.

Take other people's opinions with a grain of salt. Sure, sometimes feedback is useful, but most of the time it's not worth much.

If you ask a woman out and she says no, she's rejecting that specific moment—not your entire identity.

She doesn't know your full story or what you bring to the table. A different approach, on a different day, might have gone another way.

Value your own opinion above all. And if your opinion of yourself is low, start working on it. That's how you build real self-worth.

APPROACH ANXIETY

◆ How to Deal With Approach Anxiety:

It's normal to get anxious about starting conversations with attractive strangers.

We don't know anything about her, and our self doubts get in our own way. There's

no easy shortcut to get rid of approach anxiety. The only way to do this is through practice and repetition. There are a few things you can do to make it a bit easier though.

Breathe: Inhale deeply, then count down from 5 as you exhale. Repeat. This calms your nervous system and helps you function better.

Go out with a friend or hire a coach: Having someone with you makes approaching easier. A friend keeps you accountable, but a coach gives you expert guidance and helps you improve faster. For one-on-one coaching, visit conquerandwin.com

Take baby steps: Start small. Chat with a cashier, make a quick comment (see Challenge #3), or say hi to a few people each day. This normalizes talking to strangers.

Give yourself time: There's no rush. As long as you practice daily, you'll improve. Don't beat yourself up with "I should be good already." Everyone learns at a different pace. In my 10+ years of coaching, most guys get proficient (able to get dates) within 4–6 months, while others take longer.

Focus on opening: When you see a woman, don't overthink what comes after. Just focus on starting the conversation. Simplify.

Approach quickly: The longer you wait, the harder it gets. Anxiety builds, and she'll be gone in seconds.

Focus on what you'll gain: Instead of worrying about rejection, think about the upside —a date, a relationship, sex, a great conversation, or just valuable experience. No matter what, you win.

SIGNS SHE'S NOT INTERESTED

A lot of guys waste time and emotional energy on the wrong women. When a girl "friendzones" you, it doesn't mean that if you try harder or stick around she'll eventually be interested.

All it really means is you're losing time you could be using to meet women who are interested.

I'll dive into the full range of signs in a later book. For now, let's focus on two of the most common ones.

She Doesn't Text Back in a Reasonable Time:

Everyone's busy and you may not get a text back right away. It's not a bad sign.

A text the next day is reasonable.

But if she takes two days, three, four... days to get back to you, she's not really into you. It's easy to send a quick text even when you're busy.

She Flakes on Your Date:

When a woman really wants to meet you she'll come. If something legitimate comes up she'll reschedule. Usually right away. Otherwise, if she's going to "get back to you" it's not likely you'll hear from her.

YOUR CHALLENGES & JOURNAL

The next sections include 1 week challenges that you can use to start building your skills and confidence. Keep track of each challenge by writing notes every day and staying accountable to yourself.

After the challenge sections are completed, start writing in your journal. You can create your own challenges, and work on weaknesses. Write a little every day to stay on track and monitor progress.

YOUR CHALLENGES

CHALLENGE #1 The Eye Contact Game

Eye contact is crucial to attract women. **If you had to pick one thing to improve your game then this is it.**

Eye contact is often uncomfortable for guys who don't have a lot of confidence. Especially with attractive women.

This game will help prepare you for better conversations with attractive women. The kind of conversations which lead to dates.

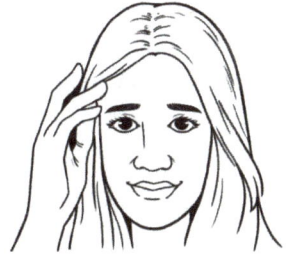

Your Challenge:

1. Go for a walk

2. Scan (see notes below) the eyes of the people passing in the other direction.

3. If someone smiles, smile back.

That's it.

YOUR CHALLENGES

Challenge #1 The Eye Contact Game

◆ Pointers for Success

If a woman makes eye contact and doesn't look away...HOLD YOUR GROUND! Whatever you do, don't look away.

If she smiles, smile back—but don't smile first. To build chemistry you need a little tension. Smiling too soon kills it. People smile to break tension, and if you do it first, you take that spark away. Let her be the one to break it when she feels the butterflies. Your job is to stand your ground and show confidence.

Don't stare: If you make eye contact and she looks away, don't stare through her. Doing so will come across overly aggressive. Continue on your way. Most of the time you'll make eye contact for a split second then it will end.

NOTE: "scanning" is not staring. It's more like a sweeping motion looking one way, then the other, stopping momentarily to lock eye contact.

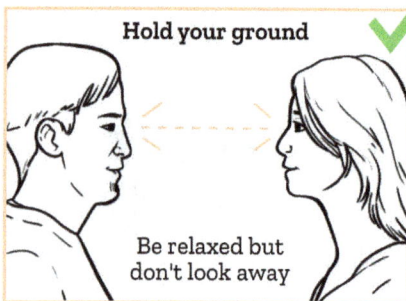

Hold your ground ✓
Be relaxed but don't look away

Only smile if she smiles first ✓

Don't stare if she looks away ✗

Continue walking if she looks away ✓

YOUR CHALLENGES

Week 1 Checklist (Eye Contact Game):

☐ Monday   ☐ Thursday   ☐ Saturday

☐ Tuesday   ☐ Friday   ☐ Sunday

☐ Wednesday

What kind of reactions are you getting from making eye contact?

_____

_____

_____

How does it feel making eye contact with strangers?

_____

_____

_____

Personal Notes & Observations:

_____

_____

_____

_____

_____

_____

_____

_____

YOUR CHALLENGES

CHALLENGE #2 Good Mornings

This exercise helps condition you to a more social lifestyle. I call it the "good morning" because you'll usually use it first thing in the day.

While walking down the street, say "good morning" as you pass people. Add a small nod, and if they smile, smile back.

At first you might speak too quietly or hesitate, which makes it easy for others to miss your greeting. Don't stress if some people don't reply—many aren't used to greeting strangers.

Just keep improving your delivery and enjoy spreading a little goodwill.

◆ **Pointers for Success**

Try eye contact (briefly) about 10 feet away but don't worry if they don't return it.

Greet them about 5 to 10 feet away so they have time to respond.

Use a STRONG voice. Do not whisper! A strong voice sounds confident

Keep the tone friendly and upbeat.

YOUR CHALLENGES

Challenge #2 Good Mornings

1. Eye contact

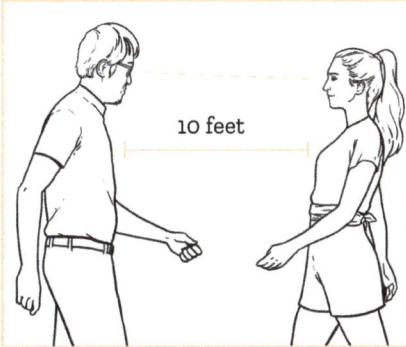

10 feet

2. Greeting

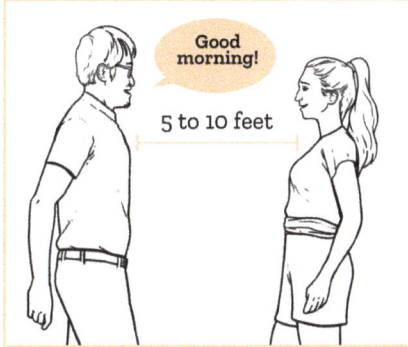

Good morning!

5 to 10 feet

3. Use a strong voice

Good morning!

Speak from your diaphragm

4. Use a friendly and upbeat tone.

Your Challenge:

1. Say hi or "good morning" to 3 people every day this week.

2. After this week's challenge is done, continue doing it every day while you complete the other challenges. Make it a part of your daily routine.

YOUR CHALLENGES

Challenge #2 Good Mornings

◆ One Week Checklist (Good Mornings):

Check off each day you complete this challenge for the first week.

- ☐ Monday
- ☐ Tuesday
- ☐ Wednesday
- ☐ Thursday
- ☐ Friday
- ☐ Saturday
- ☐ Sunday

◆ Personal Notes & Observations:

_____

_____

_____

_____

_____

_____

_____

_____

_____

CHALLENGE #3 Observational Opener

There are plenty of situations where being direct isn't the best move. Sometimes it's awkward—or flat-out inappropriate. Think of a crowded retail store, or when her boss is standing right there.

That's why it's important to have more than one approach. In these cases, you can use something I call an **"Observational Opener."**

YOUR CHALLENGES

Challenge #3 Observational Opener

This is something you can do anytime. Out on errands, shopping, getting a coffee, stopping somewhere for lunch etc.

It's less ballsy than a direct approach. It also fills in the gaps where being direct is not desirable.

It's important to have more than one "social tool" in your toolbox so you can start conversations in any scenario.

Most of the time when it works it's effortless. The woman will be the one doing most of the talking.

An observational opener is a simple comment about something in your environment.

For example, you're in a grocery store and she's looking at the soup and reading the labels.

This is something you'll see often in the grocery store. You're probably doing it too.

1. She's looking at labels trying to find the right product.
2. In a situation like this, I'll say something like, "There's too many options, it's hard to make a choice!"

This is an observation of her behavior

And they can relate to it instantly because they're in that situation right now.

That may sound like a "boring" comment because it is. But here's a fact: **you don't need an interesting comment to start a conversation.**

YOUR CHALLENGES

Challenge #3 Observational Opener

◆ Don't Try to Be "Interesting"

Many guys will lose opportunities because they think they have to say something "interesting". All you have to do is say 'something' with a smile on your face, and confidence in your voice.

One mistake guys make is thinking they need something interesting to say (or smart, funny, witty etc.).

What happens when guys try to think of something interesting to say is that they don't say anything. The moment of opportunity will pass while a guy is trying to come up with a "great opener".

Of course, to get a date you'll have to change the topic. I'll cover how to create a meaningful conversation shortly.

What you say is only one part of starting a conversation. More important is how you say it.

You have to have intent. Don't talk to everyone as if you're their friend. Feel your attraction for her and avoid suppressing your feelings to look like a "nice guy".

If you feel your sexual desire for her you'll subtly express the right things. Your voice, body language and eye contact will work together.

A lot of guys who get "friend-zoned" suppress their attraction for women trying to look like a "nice guy". This sabotages their attempts to attract women.

YOUR CHALLENGES

Challenge #3 Observational Opener

TIP: This isn't about sending overt signals to her. It's about allowing your full range of emotional expression. The more confident you are, the easier this will become.

This is the hardest thing for guys to learn, but as you get more experience it will start to "click" and require less effort.

So, let's begin.

Pointers for Success

- Keep these points in mind when you go out. **Don't expect anything from any woman you talk to:** Just focus on the action of making an observation. This will keep you from becoming disappointed or putting too much pressure on yourself.

- **Do it daily:** To get dates from starting "random" conversations you'll need to be consistent. Doing it occasionally won't allow you to get good at this or create opportunities for dates.

- **Stay relaxed:** It's just a casual comment, so don't sweat it. The more relaxed you are the better it will work.

- **Smile and be playful:** Just like being relaxed, smiling when you talk to women will get better responses. We all react positively to a sincere smile, so show your shiny whites.

- **Don't force any conversation:** If you talk to someone who comes across disinterested or distracted, don't try to continue.

YOUR CHALLENGES

Challenge #3 Observational Opener

◆ What to expect

The majority of the time you'll get a response. For example, you comment, "It's hard to find anything here!" Her: "That's right, it is!" - Usually this is where it will end.

She'll continue doing what she was doing. This is OK. Focus on being social, and don't worry about these conversations going further.

◆ How to open with an observation

In a shopping scenario:

Place yourself nearby, facing the products you're looking at. Turn your head towards her and make an observation with a smile on your face. **Pay attention to her reaction.** If it's positive or talkative, continue. If she's brief and keeps going about her business, don't continue.

Body Language:

- ✓ **Plant yourself nearby,** but not in her personal bubble (4-6 feet away).
- ✓ **Stay parallel to her.** Don't turn to face her or even angle in at 45 degrees. Remember—you're just shopping, not "approaching."
- ✓ **Turn your head towards her when you speak.** This is important so your voice is projected to her.
- ✓ **Speak to be heard.** Don't get quiet when you speak to women. She may not hear you. Even if she does, a quiet voice doesn't sound confident.

See examples on the next page

YOUR CHALLENGES

Challenge #3 Observational Opener

1. Plant yourself nearby

Don't enter her personal bubble

Stay 4-6 feet away

2. Stay Parallel to her

Face the shelves

Don't turn to face her (Too aggressive)

3. Turn your head to speak to her

Those are really good

4. Speak to be heard

YOUR CHALLENGES

Challenge #3 Observational Opener

◆ Some Examples

Here are some examples from different scenarios which you can try out.

- ✅ She's looking at some steaks, "It looks like you have a system to figure out which steak is best".

- ✅ If she keeps grabbing items off the shelf then putting them back, "It's hard to find the right thing sometimes!"

- ✅ In a lineup at a cafe, "These lines always take forever when you're trying to get your first coffee! Maybe it's a caffeine time warp?"

- ✅ In a busy cafe or shop, "It's so loud in here, it sounds like a club!"

- ✅ In a quiet shop, "It's so quiet in here, it sounds like a library."

- ✅ Seated in a cafe, a girl seated nearby who's studying, "That looks like some heavy reading! What are you studying?"

And many more. The key here is **NOT** to remember any lines. **Pay attention to your surroundings and make a simple comment.** That's it. This way you can adapt to any situation.

◆ Question Openers

Sometimes it's easiest to ask a question. **Some questions you can ask:**

- ✅ Which one is the best?
- ✅ Is that any good?
- ✅ What do you use that for?
- ✅ What are you studying?

The observations and questions above are only a starting point. They don't cover every possible thing you could say. Use them as examples to get going, then practice in real life and develop your own.

REMEMBER: HOW you say it is more important than WHAT you say.

YOUR CHALLENGES

Challenge #3 Observational Opener

◆ Observational Opener Examples

She's looking at some steaks

It looks like you have a system to figure out which steak is best

If she keeps grabbing items off the shelf then putting them back

It's hard to find the right thing sometimes!

In a lineup at a cafe

These lines always take forever when you're trying to get your first coffee! Maybe it's a caffeine time warp?

MAKE A COMMENT THAT IS RELEVANT TO HER. YOU CAN SAY ALMOST ANYTHING BUT DON'T MAKE IT ABOUT YOURSELF. PEOPLE ARE MUCH MORE LIKELY TO RESPOND WHEN IT'S ABOUT THEMSELVES (OR SOMETHING THEY ARE EXPERIENCING TOO, LIKE THE ENVIRONMENT)

YOUR CHALLENGES

Challenge #3 Observational Opener

◆ The Conversation

Hi

*Refer to the section on making conversations for full details.

Before asking her out, it's important to learn about her. If you jump from small talk about the weather to suddenly asking her out, it will be out of place.

By getting her to share about herself, you will make it feel natural when you ask her out. Talking about ourselves builds trust and chemistry.

If she opens up with something personal, she doesn't really "know" you yet—but it feels like she does. And in dating, feelings matter more than logic.

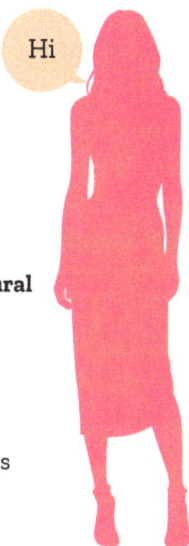

> If you make her *feel something* she'll want to see you again. If the right feeling isn't there then nothing will make her interested.

To turn a simple observation into a meaningful conversation, you need to bridge topics.

Pay close attention to what she says—people naturally drop little details in casual conversation.

For example, if you start talking about the weather and she says, "Yeah, I have to buy an umbrella for my mother before she gets here..."—that's your opening to move the conversation forward.

YOUR CHALLENGES

Challenge #3 Observational Opener

Now it's easy to bridge the topic. You can ask, "Oh, is your family visiting—where from?" That shifts the conversation from small talk to something more personal.

From there, you can ask: "Where are they visiting from?" → "Are you originally from [city]?" → "What brought you here?"

Each question opens her up more and builds a natural connection by focusing on her life and experiences.

You can also bridge by asking about whatever she's holding, buying, or doing: "What are you getting that for?"

PAY ATTENTION: Avoid interrogating her by breaking up questions with statements. Example: Oh, I always thought these were for doing X things etc.

> I saw a woman looking at shower heads in a hardware store and asked her if she was doing a renovation. That simple question led to a conversation about her project, which shifted into talking about her work and interests. Later, we met up and went on a date.

So listen for:

- ✅ Personal details.
- ✅ Anything about what she's doing during the day.
- ✅ Anything about what she's using a product for.
- ✅ What she's up to.
- ✅ What she likes or dislikes.
- ✅ An accent.

Then follow up with a question about any of the above to get her to open up more. This will help develop a full conversation.

YOUR CHALLENGES

Challenge #3 Observational Opener

REMEMBER:

Do not turn towards her. This shows too much intent and may repel her or create awkwardness.

Asking Her Out / When you ask her out:

1. Look in her eyes.

2. Use a strong voice (don't get quiet!).

3. Be assertive by using assertive language.

4. Don't fidget or put your hands in your pockets.

Use an assertive statement like, "**Let's have a coffee sometime.**" or "**We should have a coffee sometime.**"

Never use passive language. Passive language doesn't sound confident.

Examples include: "Do you want to...?" "Would you like to...?" "Can we....?" etc. Usually this kind of language is used with a passive, soft voice.

When asking women out, assume the answer is "yes" and speak confidently like a man who expects a yes.

This doesn't guarantee she'll say yes. But like everything else, it will help increase your odds.

YOUR CHALLENGES

Challenge #3 Observational Opener

◆ **Asking her out example**

Do This

Let's have a coffee sometime

1. Look in her eyes. ✓
2. Use a strong voice (don't get quiet!). ✓
3. Be assertive by using assertive language. ✓
4. Don't fidget or put your hands in your pockets. ✓

Don't Do This

Can we have a coffee sometime?

1. Avoiding eye contact. ✗
2. Quiet voice. ✗
3. Passive language. ✗
4. Hands in pockets. ✗

YOUR CHALLENGES

Challenge #3 Observational Opener

Your Challenge

Don't worry about remembering every detail you've just read—it takes repetition to really sink in.

Pick a date to start this challenge, then plan at least one outing every day that week to practice. Use the checklist on the next page to track your progress.

It doesn't matter which day you start. Write the date beside it and complete all seven days in a row.

I will start day one on:

Now, choose a location where you'll try. Pick a grocery store, cafe, shopping mall etc. I will go to _____ and make one observational opener OR question opener.

◆ One Week Checklist (Observational Openers):

- ☐ Monday
- ☐ Tuesday
- ☐ Wednesday
- ☐ Thursday
- ☐ Friday
- ☐ Saturday
- ☐ Sunday

◆ What kind of reaction did you get from making your comment/question?

_____

_____

_____

YOUR CHALLENGES

◆ **What was one thing which could be improved? (voice, eye contact, body language, your question/observation etc)**

_____

_____

_____

◆ **Personal Notes & Observations:**

_____

_____

_____

_____

_____

_____

_____

_____

◆ **What was one good thing about your opener? (a smile, strong voice, good observation etc.**

_____

_____

_____

YOUR CHALLENGES

Challenge #4 The Direct Approach

Gain

- New social skills.
- The ability to overcome your inner fears and take action.
- The ability to be assertive (a quality which is attractive to women and respected by men).

- The art of persuasion.
- A more outgoing personality.
- Character development (Learn how to handle pressure, think fast, handle different personalities).

And much more.

Your Challenge:

Learn the steps below, and set a day to go out and approach a woman directly. Don't worry about getting a phone number, just give a sincere compliment and a smile.

◆ How approach a woman walking down the street:

1. **Get her attention:** Walk up beside her (outside of her personal bubble) and say "excuse me" as if you're asking for directions.

2. **Use a "mini story" (see next page) immediately after opening.** Just blurting out compliments doesn't work well.

Many women will react by walking away. With a "mini story" you'll have her full attention and curiosity before you tell her why you approached. This will help get more consistent, positive results.

3. **Give her a simple compliment:** The key here is to give a sincere compliment which doesn't go overboard. The best compliments aren't too aggressive. "I thought you looked great!" or "You look nice." or "You have a nice sense of style." all work well.

YOUR CHALLENGES

Challenge #4 The Direct Approach

1. Walk up beside her

2. Get her attention

Excuse me!

3. Use a Mini story 4. Give her a simple compliment

I was going the other way, on the way to meet a buddy when I noticed you, and I had to come back here to say hi because you look great.

Things to pay attention to:

1. **Smile.**

2. **Be enthusiastic:** Enthusiasm is contagious and will hold people's attention. A monotone voice will act like a social repellent.

3. **Speak with a strong voice:** A quiet voice sounds insecure. Speak like a boss.

4. **If she doesn't stop, do not follow:** Always give the women you approach an easy exit if they don't want to chat.

5. **Give her space:** If you can stretch your arm out and can't touch her, that's a good distance. Nobody likes it when a stranger invades their personal space.

YOUR CHALLENGES

Challenge #4 The Direct Approach

1. SMILE ✅

2. BE ENTHUSIASTIC ✅

3. USE A STRONG VOICE ✅

4. DO NOT FOLLOW HER ❌

5. STAY OUT OF HER PERSONAL SPACE ✅

YOUR CHALLENGES

◆ The "mini story"

The **mini story** is about **painting a picture and grabbing her attention**. It sparks curiosity, cuts through distractions, and avoids canned-sounding lines. All you do is tell her exactly what was happening right before you approached.

For example:
"Excuse me, I was heading to lunch and wasn't sure if I should do this. I'm already late, but I saw you walking by, so I ran back across the street—dodged traffic and even a tiny chihuahua—just to say hi because you look great."

Now you've got her full attention, and your compliment comes across as genuine.

> **Keep in mind:**
>
> **Tell her exactly what was happening before you approached.** If you were walking up the street to meet your friends for lunch, tell her that. If you were just heading home after a long day of work, that's your "story".
>
> **Your mini story should always be true:** Never lie. It doesn't matter if what you were doing wasn't interesting. The mini story is just to get her attention and create a moment to start a conversation.

By painting a picture for her she'll follow along and get curious where your story is leading. This is the 'hook' that will keep her attention and smoothly transition to your reason for approaching.

> **NOTE: This 'direct approach' can be adapted to any situation**, whether she is standing at a bus stop or walking in a mall etc. Change your mini-story to fit the situation. *You do not need to make eye contact first.

YOUR CHALLENGES

Challenge #4 The Direct Approach

What is the best way to meet women in groups?

Approaching a group of women can be intimidating for guys. Instead of dealing with one attractive woman, you've got her friends staring at you too.

When you start, focus on single women. If you want a bigger challenge then follow the steps in the next page.

Here's how to meet groups of women (2 or more)

1. **Get their attention:** Just like stopping one woman, start with "excuse me." Make eye contact with each girl in the group
2. **Focus on the woman you want:** Put your attention on the woman you want. Glance at her friend(s) too to keep their attention.
3. **Go direct:** Use a compliment opener like, "I saw you walk by and liked your style. I had to come back and say hi."
4. **Acknowledge her friends:** Look back at her friends to acknowledge their presence. "Sorry to interrupt but your friend caught my attention."
5. **Compliment the whole group:** If they're all cute then do the above steps for the whole group. You can decide who you want to ask out after you decide who you like best.

YOUR CHALLENGES

Challenge #4 The Direct Approach

1. Get their attention

Excuse me! Make eye contact with all of them.

2. Focus on the woman you want

3. Go direct

I saw you walk by and liked your style. I had to come back and say hi.

4. Acknowledge her friends:

Smile at them

5. Opener Variation: Compliment the group (if they're all cute)

I thought you guys look great!

YOUR CHALLENGES

Getting Her Number

How to get her phone number

1. **Ask her out for coffee or a drink:** This works better than asking for her number first. She'll be focused on the outing instead of her phone number. After a good conversation, say, "We should grab a coffee sometime."

2. **Get her number:** Keep talking as you pull your phone out, then ask, "What's your number?"

Pointers for Success

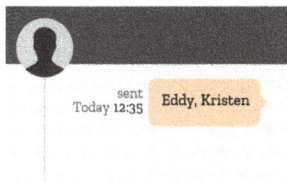

sent
Today 12:35   Eddy, Kristen

Always send her a text while she's still standing in front of you. Add her name so you remember who she is, and include your name so she knows who you are. That way, when you text her later, there's no awkward "Who's this?" moment.

Some notes on texting her

After you get her number, how do you set up a date?

Here are some rules of thumb:

1. Don't text your life story
2. Don't try to "create interest" by text—if you did your job when you met her, she's already interested.
3. Set up the date the same day you meet. Women forget quickly how they felt in the moment, and their interest fades.
4. Keep it simple: "Hi Jenny, nice running into you today :) Let's grab a drink later this week. What day works for you?"

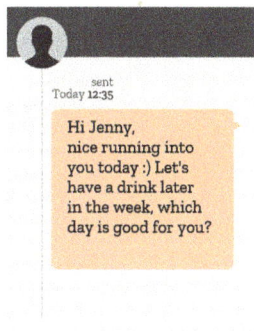

sent
Today 12:35

Hi Jenny, nice running into you today :) Let's have a drink later in the week, which day is good for you?

YOUR CHALLENGES

◆ The Conversation

Your job in a conversation is to lead it in the right direction so you can learn about her. Never chat without a purpose.

To do that use the **snowball technique.**

The basic format: ask a "what" question, then a "why" question.

1. **Talk about her.** People like talking about themselves.
2. **Start with "what."** "What do you do?" "What are you working on?"
3. **Find out "Why":** Now ask her "why" she does what she does. This part is crucial. Superficial conversations won't create a connection. Example: "What inspired you to get into that?" or "Why did you decide to get into this field?"
4. **Dig deeper.** Stay on the topic while it's alive; ask simple follow-ups about her story before switching subjects.

◆ Pointers for Success

• **Prevent an 'interview' by adding your opinion:** If you keep asking questions without breaking it up, it will get boring quickly.

When she tells you what she does, first add your opinion on the topic, "You're a nurse? I've heard it can be stressful. Nurses are always dealing with sick people and long hours." Then finish with your "why" question: "Why did you get into nursing?"

YOUR CHALLENGES

The Conversation

Conversation steps

1. Ask a "what" question 2. Listen to her carefully

3. Give your opinion 4. Find out "why" she got into her field

YOUR CHALLENGES

The Conversation

Why It Works

When people share something meaningful, it builds trust and chemistry. Work is often tied to identity—many people spend years in school or training to enter their field.

Even if her current job isn't significant, there's usually a story behind it.
You can also ask, "What would you do if you could do anything?" to uncover her real passions.

Jumping from subject to subject keeps the conversation shallow and blocks real connection. Stick with one topic long enough to go deeper.

◆ Will Women Reject Me If I Approach in a Public Space?

Few women will respond rudely to a sincere approach. The worst reaction is getting ignored. They'll just keep walking or say they're busy.

Many guys are trying to "not lose" instead of trying to win. You can't win if you're always focused on how women might reject you.

> Keep your eyes on the prize to get the best results. When guys focus on what they don't want they have a tendency to make it happen.

Which day/time will you go out to try being direct?

Date: Time:

YOUR CHALLENGES

Some questions for self reflection:

☐ Have you tried going direct?　　☐ What happened?

_____
_____
_____
_____
_____
_____

◆ **What's ONE thing you did which was good?**

_____
_____
_____

◆ **What's ONE thig which could be better?**

_____
_____
_____

◆ **One Week Checklist (Direct):**

☐ Monday　　☐ Wednesday　　☐ Friday　　☐ Sunday

☐ Tuesday　　☐ Thursday　　☐ Saturday

ALWAYS FRAME YOUR EXPERIENCES IN A POSITIVE LIGHT. NEVER PUT YOURSELF DOWN BECAUSE YOU DIDN'T LIKE THE WAY IT WENT. YOU CAN GIVE YOURSELF CREDIT BECAUSE YOU TRIED.

WHAT'S NEXT?

You've made it this far, congrats.

Don't stop here. Use your journal to track every experience and measure your progress.

Stay accountable by setting a schedule to go out and practice regularly.

In part two of this series, I'll show you exactly what to do on your dates and how to turn them into real relationships.

Want one on one coaching? Go to conquerandwin.com

My Goals:

Write down your main goals and challenges here. In the journal you will be able to write daily and monthly goals, and keep track of progress.

My main dating goal is:

_____

_____

My main relationship goal is:

_____

_____

My biggest challenge to achieve my goals is (confidence, body language, fear of rejection, conversation skills etc):

_____

_____

BONUS EXERCISES:

If the being direct is difficult for you these will make it easier.

A. NOT a Starbucks exercise:

Ask an attractive woman on the street: Do you know where there is a coffee shop which is NOT a Starbucks?

*Work on how you use your voice. Make it humorous by emphasizing "NOT". You'll get a laugh from some women if done well.

This will teach you all the steps you'd normally take to be direct without the adrenaline. You'll also get practice talking to women and could get a date.

B. Walk into a store with an attractive cashier:

Ask her a question about the product or service they offer.

THEN, try to bridge your conversation into something about her (See P.51).

NOTE: Don't force the topic. Wait for her to say something you can bridge into something more personal.

90 DAY JOURNAL

This journal has been set to 90 days to help keep yourself accountable long enough to learn some new skills and create some new habits. The more consistent you are the faster you'll develop your lifestyle habits and confidence.

JOURNAL

For personalized coaching: conquerandwin.com

Date: **Day #**

End of the day summary:

How many women did you chat with today?

How many women did you ask out on dates?

I reframed negative thoughts into positive thoughts: **Y/N**

Tomorrow's goals: Write your list each day

_____ ☐
_____ ☐
_____ ☐
_____

Personal Notes & Observations:

_____
_____
_____
_____
_____
_____
_____
_____

JOURNAL

For personalized coaching: conquerandwin.com

Date: **Day #**

End of the day summary:

How many women did you chat with today?

How many women did you ask out on dates?

I reframed negative thoughts into positive thoughts: **Y/N**

Tomorrow's goals: Write your list each day

_____ ☐
_____ ☐
_____ ☐

Personal Notes & Observations:

_____
_____
_____
_____
_____
_____
_____
_____

JOURNAL

For personalized coaching: conquerandwin.com

Date: **Day #**

End of the day summary:

How many women did you chat with today?

How many women did you ask out on dates?

I reframed negative thoughts into positive thoughts: **Y/N**

Tomorrow's goals: Write your list each day

- ☐ _____
- ☐ _____
- ☐ _____

Personal Notes & Observations:

_____
_____
_____
_____
_____
_____
_____
_____
_____

JOURNAL

For personalized coaching: conquerandwin.com

Date: **Day #**

End of the day summary:

How many women did you chat with today?

How many women did you ask out on dates?

I reframed negative thoughts into positive thoughts: **Y/N**

Tomorrow's goals: Write your list each day

☐
_____
☐
_____
☐
_____

Personal Notes & Observations:

_____
_____
_____
_____
_____
_____
_____
_____

JOURNAL

For personalized coaching: conquerandwin.com

Date: **Day #**

End of the day summary:

How many women did you chat with today?

How many women did you ask out on dates?

I reframed negative thoughts into positive thoughts: **Y/N**

Tomorrow's goals: Write your list each day

_____ ☐
_____ ☐
_____ ☐
_____

Personal Notes & Observations:

_____
_____
_____
_____
_____
_____
_____
_____

JOURNAL

For personalized coaching: conquerandwin.com

Date: **Day #**

End of the day summary:

How many women did you chat with today?

How many women did you ask out on dates?

I reframed negative thoughts into positive thoughts: **Y/N**

Tomorrow's goals: Write your list each day

☐
_____
☐
_____
☐
_____

Personal Notes & Observations:

_____
_____
_____
_____
_____
_____
_____
_____

JOURNAL

For personalized coaching: conquerandwin.com

Date: **Day #**

End of the day summary:

How many women did you chat with today?

How many women did you ask out on dates?

I reframed negative thoughts into positive thoughts: **Y/N**

Tomorrow's goals: Write your list each day

☐
_____
☐
_____
☐
_____

Personal Notes & Observations:

_____
_____
_____
_____
_____
_____
_____
_____

JOURNAL

For personalized coaching: conquerandwin.com

Date: **Day #**

End of the day summary:

How many women did you chat with today?

How many women did you ask out on dates?

I reframed negative thoughts into positive thoughts: **Y/N**

Tomorrow's goals: Write your list each day

☐
☐
☐

Personal Notes & Observations:

JOURNAL

For personalized coaching: conquerandwin.com

Date: **Day #**

End of the day summary:

How many women did you chat with today?

How many women did you ask out on dates?

I reframed negative thoughts into positive thoughts: **Y/N**

Tomorrow's goals: Write your list each day

_____ ☐
_____ ☐
_____ ☐
_____

Personal Notes & Observations:

_____
_____
_____
_____
_____
_____
_____
_____

JOURNAL

For personalized coaching: conquerandwin.com

Date: **Day #**

End of the day summary:

How many women did you chat with today?

How many women did you ask out on dates?

I reframed negative thoughts into positive thoughts: **Y/N**

Tomorrow's goals: Write your list each day

☐
_____
_____
☐
_____
☐

Personal Notes & Observations:

_____
_____
_____
_____
_____
_____
_____
_____

JOURNAL

For personalized coaching: conquerandwin.com

Date: **Day #**

End of the day summary:

How many women did you chat with today?

How many women did you ask out on dates?

I reframed negative thoughts into positive thoughts: **Y/N**

Tomorrow's goals: Write your list each day

_____ ☐
_____ ☐
_____ ☐

Personal Notes & Observations:

_____
_____
_____
_____
_____
_____
_____
_____

JOURNAL

For personalized coaching: conquerandwin.com

Date: **Day #**

End of the day summary:

How many women did you chat with today?

How many women did you ask out on dates?

I reframed negative thoughts into positive thoughts: **Y/N**

Tomorrow's goals: Write your list each day

☐
_____
☐
_____
☐
_____

Personal Notes & Observations:

_____
_____
_____
_____
_____
_____
_____

JOURNAL

For personalized coaching: conquerandwin.com

Date: **Day #**

End of the day summary:

How many women did you chat with today?

How many women did you ask out on dates?

I reframed negative thoughts into positive thoughts: **Y/N**

Tomorrow's goals: Write your list each day

_____ ☐
_____ ☐
_____ ☐
_____

Personal Notes & Observations:

_____
_____
_____
_____
_____
_____
_____
_____

JOURNAL

For personalized coaching: conquerandwin.com

Date: **Day #**

End of the day summary:

How many women did you chat with today?

How many women did you ask out on dates?

I reframed negative thoughts into positive thoughts: **Y/N**

Tomorrow's goals: Write your list each day

_____ ☐
_____ ☐
_____ ☐

Personal Notes & Observations:

_____
_____
_____
_____
_____
_____
_____
_____

JOURNAL

For personalized coaching: conquerandwin.com

Date: **Day #**

End of the day summary:

How many women did you chat with today?

How many women did you ask out on dates?

I reframed negative thoughts into positive thoughts: **Y/N**

Tomorrow's goals: Write your list each day

☐
_____
☐
_____
☐
_____

Personal Notes & Observations:

_____
_____
_____
_____
_____
_____
_____
_____

JOURNAL

For personalized coaching: conquerandwin.com

Date: **Day #**

End of the day summary:

How many women did you chat with today?

How many women did you ask out on dates?

I reframed negative thoughts into positive thoughts: **Y/N**

Tomorrow's goals: Write your list each day

☐
_____
☐
_____
☐
_____

Personal Notes & Observations:

_____
_____
_____
_____
_____
_____
_____
_____

JOURNAL

For personalized coaching: conquerandwin.com

Date: **Day #**

End of the day summary:

How many women did you chat with today?

How many women did you ask out on dates?

I reframed negative thoughts into positive thoughts: **Y/N**

Tomorrow's goals: Write your list each day

☐
_____
☐
_____
☐
_____

Personal Notes & Observations:

_____
_____
_____
_____
_____
_____
_____
_____

JOURNAL

For personalized coaching: conquerandwin.com

Date: **Day #**

End of the day summary:

How many women did you chat with today?

How many women did you ask out on dates?

I reframed negative thoughts into positive thoughts: **Y/N**

Tomorrow's goals: Write your list each day

- [ ]
- [ ]
- [ ]

Personal Notes & Observations:

_____
_____
_____
_____
_____
_____
_____
_____

JOURNAL

For personalized coaching: conquerandwin.com

Date: **Day #**

End of the day summary:

How many women did you chat with today?

How many women did you ask out on dates?

I reframed negative thoughts into positive thoughts: **Y/N**

Tomorrow's goals: Write your list each day

_____ ☐
_____ ☐
_____ ☐
_____

Personal Notes & Observations:

_____
_____
_____
_____
_____
_____
_____
_____

JOURNAL

For personalized coaching: conquerandwin.com

Date: **Day #**

End of the day summary:

How many women did you chat with today?

How many women did you ask out on dates?

I reframed negative thoughts into positive thoughts: **Y/N**

Tomorrow's goals: Write your list each day

☐
_____
_____ ☐
_____
_____ ☐

Personal Notes & Observations:

_____
_____
_____
_____
_____
_____
_____
_____

JOURNAL

For personalized coaching: conquerandwin.com

Date: **Day #**

End of the day summary:

How many women did you chat with today?

How many women did you ask out on dates?

I reframed negative thoughts into positive thoughts: **Y/N**

Tomorrow's goals: Write your list each day

☐
_____
☐
_____
☐
_____
_____

Personal Notes & Observations:

_____
_____
_____
_____
_____
_____
_____
_____

JOURNAL

For personalized coaching: conquerandwin.com

Date: **Day #**

End of the day summary:

How many women did you chat with today?

How many women did you ask out on dates?

I reframed negative thoughts into positive thoughts: **Y/N**

Tomorrow's goals: Write your list each day

_____ ☐
_____ ☐
_____ ☐

Personal Notes & Observations:

_____
_____
_____
_____
_____
_____
_____
_____

JOURNAL

For personalized coaching: conquerandwin.com

Date: **Day #**

End of the day summary:

How many women did you chat with today?

How many women did you ask out on dates?

I reframed negative thoughts into positive thoughts: **Y/N**

Tomorrow's goals: Write your list each day

☐
_____
☐
_____
☐
_____

Personal Notes & Observations:

_____
_____
_____
_____
_____
_____
_____
_____

JOURNAL

For personalized coaching: conquerandwin.com

Date: **Day #**

End of the day summary:

How many women did you chat with today?

How many women did you ask out on dates?

I reframed negative thoughts into positive thoughts: **Y/N**

Tomorrow's goals: Write your list each day

☐
☐
☐

Personal Notes & Observations:

JOURNAL

For personalized coaching: conquerandwin.com

Date: **Day #**

End of the day summary:

How many women did you chat with today?

How many women did you ask out on dates?

I reframed negative thoughts into positive thoughts: **Y/N**

Tomorrow's goals: Write your list each day

☐
_____
☐
_____
☐
_____

Personal Notes & Observations:

_____
_____
_____
_____
_____
_____
_____
_____

90 day journal

JOURNAL

For personalized coaching: conquerandwin.com

Date: **Day #**

End of the day summary:

How many women did you chat with today?

How many women did you ask out on dates?

I reframed negative thoughts into positive thoughts: **Y/N**

Tomorrow's goals: Write your list each day

- [ ]
- [ ]
- [ ]

Personal Notes & Observations:

JOURNAL

For personalized coaching: conquerandwin.com

Date: **Day #**

End of the day summary:

How many women did you chat with today?

How many women did you ask out on dates?

I reframed negative thoughts into positive thoughts: **Y/N**

Tomorrow's goals: Write your list each day

☐
_____
☐
_____
☐
_____

Personal Notes & Observations:

_____
_____
_____
_____
_____
_____
_____
_____

JOURNAL

For personalized coaching: conquerandwin.com

Date: **Day #**

End of the day summary:

How many women did you chat with today?

How many women did you ask out on dates?

I reframed negative thoughts into positive thoughts: **Y/N**

Tomorrow's goals: Write your list each day

_____ ☐
_____ ☐
_____ ☐

Personal Notes & Observations:

_____
_____
_____
_____
_____
_____
_____
_____

JOURNAL

For personalized coaching: conquerandwin.com

Date: **Day #**

End of the day summary:

How many women did you chat with today?

How many women did you ask out on dates?

I reframed negative thoughts into positive thoughts: **Y/N**

Tomorrow's goals: Write your list each day

_____ ☐
_____ ☐
_____ ☐

Personal Notes & Observations:

_____
_____
_____
_____
_____
_____
_____
_____

JOURNAL

For personalized coaching: conquerandwin.com

Date: **Day #**

End of the day summary:

How many women did you chat with today?

How many women did you ask out on dates?

I reframed negative thoughts into positive thoughts: **Y/N**

Tomorrow's goals: Write your list each day

☐
_____

☐
_____

☐
_____

Personal Notes & Observations:

_____
_____
_____
_____
_____
_____
_____
_____

MONTHLY REVIEW:

◆ **How I rate this month overall:**

_____

_____

◆ **What did I learn this month?**

_____

_____

_____

_____

_____

My biggest accomplishment is:

_____

_____

_____

◆ **What will I Improve in the next 30 days?**

_____

_____

_____

_____

_____

JOURNAL

For personalized coaching: conquerandwin.com

Date: **Day #**

End of the day summary:

How many women did you chat with today?

How many women did you ask out on dates?

I reframed negative thoughts into positive thoughts: **Y/N**

Tomorrow's goals: Write your list each day

☐
_____
☐
_____
☐
_____

Personal Notes & Observations:

_____
_____
_____
_____
_____
_____
_____
_____

JOURNAL

For personalized coaching: conquerandwin.com

Date: **Day #**

End of the day summary:

How many women did you chat with today?

How many women did you ask out on dates?

I reframed negative thoughts into positive thoughts: **Y/N**

Tomorrow's goals: Write your list each day

☐
_____
☐
_____
☐
_____

Personal Notes & Observations:

_____
_____
_____
_____
_____
_____
_____
_____

JOURNAL

For personalized coaching: conquerandwin.com

Date: **Day #**

End of the day summary:

How many women did you chat with today?

How many women did you ask out on dates?

I reframed negative thoughts into positive thoughts: **Y/N**

Tomorrow's goals: Write your list each day

☐

☐

☐

Personal Notes & Observations:

JOURNAL

For personalized coaching: conquerandwin.com

Date: **Day #**

End of the day summary:

How many women did you chat with today?

How many women did you ask out on dates?

I reframed negative thoughts into positive thoughts: **Y/N**

Tomorrow's goals: Write your list each day

☐

☐

☐

Personal Notes & Observations:

JOURNAL

For personalized coaching: conquerandwin.com

Date: **Day #**

End of the day summary:

How many women did you chat with today?

How many women did you ask out on dates?

I reframed negative thoughts into positive thoughts: **Y/N**

Tomorrow's goals: Write your list each day

- [ ] _____
- [ ] _____
- [ ] _____

Personal Notes & Observations:

_____
_____
_____
_____
_____
_____
_____
_____

JOURNAL

For personalized coaching: conquerandwin.com

Date: **Day #**

End of the day summary:

How many women did you chat with today?

How many women did you ask out on dates?

I reframed negative thoughts into positive thoughts: **Y/N**

Tomorrow's goals: Write your list each day

_____ ☐
_____ ☐
_____ ☐

Personal Notes & Observations:

_____
_____
_____
_____
_____
_____
_____
_____

JOURNAL

For personalized coaching: conquerandwin.com

Date: **Day #**

End of the day summary:

How many women did you chat with today?

How many women did you ask out on dates?

I reframed negative thoughts into positive thoughts: **Y/N**

Tomorrow's goals: Write your list each day

- ☐ _____
- ☐ _____
- ☐ _____

Personal Notes & Observations:

_____
_____
_____
_____
_____
_____
_____
_____

JOURNAL

For personalized coaching: conquerandwin.com

Date: **Day #**

End of the day summary:

How many women did you chat with today?

How many women did you ask out on dates?

I reframed negative thoughts into positive thoughts: **Y/N**

Tomorrow's goals: Write your list each day

☐
_____
☐
_____
☐
_____

Personal Notes & Observations:

_____
_____
_____
_____
_____
_____
_____
_____

JOURNAL

For personalized coaching: conquerandwin.com

Date: **Day #**

End of the day summary:

How many women did you chat with today?

How many women did you ask out on dates?

I reframed negative thoughts into positive thoughts: **Y/N**

Tomorrow's goals: Write your list each day

- ☐ _____
- ☐ _____
- ☐ _____

Personal Notes & Observations:

_____
_____
_____
_____
_____
_____
_____
_____

JOURNAL

For personalized coaching: conquerandwin.com

Date: **Day #**

End of the day summary:

How many women did you chat with today?

How many women did you ask out on dates?

I reframed negative thoughts into positive thoughts: **Y/N**

Tomorrow's goals: Write your list each day

_____ ☐
_____ ☐
_____ ☐
_____

Personal Notes & Observations:

_____
_____
_____
_____
_____
_____
_____
_____
_____

JOURNAL

For personalized coaching: conquerandwin.com

Date: **Day #**

End of the day summary:

How many women did you chat with today?

How many women did you ask out on dates?

I reframed negative thoughts into positive thoughts: **Y/N**

Tomorrow's goals: Write your list each day

☐

_____

☐

_____

☐

_____

Personal Notes & Observations:

_____

_____

_____

_____

_____

_____

_____

_____

JOURNAL

For personalized coaching: conquerandwin.com

Date: **Day #**

End of the day summary:

How many women did you chat with today?

How many women did you ask out on dates?

I reframed negative thoughts into positive thoughts: **Y/N**

Tomorrow's goals: Write your list each day

_____ ☐
_____ ☐
_____ ☐

Personal Notes & Observations:

_____
_____
_____
_____
_____
_____
_____
_____

JOURNAL

For personalized coaching: conquerandwin.com

Date: **Day #**

End of the day summary:

How many women did you chat with today?

How many women did you ask out on dates?

I reframed negative thoughts into positive thoughts: **Y/N**

Tomorrow's goals: Write your list each day

- ☐ _____
- ☐ _____
- ☐ _____

Personal Notes & Observations:

_____

_____

_____

_____

_____

_____

_____

_____

JOURNAL

For personalized coaching: conquerandwin.com

Date: **Day #**

End of the day summary:

How many women did you chat with today?

How many women did you ask out on dates?

I reframed negative thoughts into positive thoughts: **Y/N**

Tomorrow's goals: Write your list each day

_____ ☐
_____ ☐
_____ ☐

Personal Notes & Observations:

_____
_____
_____
_____
_____
_____
_____
_____

JOURNAL

For personalized coaching: conquerandwin.com

Date: **Day #**

End of the day summary:

How many women did you chat with today?

How many women did you ask out on dates?

I reframed negative thoughts into positive thoughts: **Y/N**

Tomorrow's goals: Write your list each day

☐
_____
☐
_____
☐
_____

Personal Notes & Observations:

_____
_____
_____
_____
_____
_____
_____
_____

JOURNAL

For personalized coaching: conquerandwin.com

Date: **Day #**

End of the day summary:

How many women did you chat with today?

How many women did you ask out on dates?

I reframed negative thoughts into positive thoughts: **Y/N**

Tomorrow's goals: Write your list each day

_____ ☐
_____ ☐
_____ ☐

Personal Notes & Observations:

_____
_____
_____
_____
_____
_____
_____
_____

JOURNAL

For personalized coaching: conquerandwin.com

Date: **Day #**

End of the day summary:

How many women did you chat with today?

How many women did you ask out on dates?

I reframed negative thoughts into positive thoughts: **Y/N**

Tomorrow's goals: Write your list each day

☐
☐
☐

Personal Notes & Observations:

JOURNAL

For personalized coaching: conquerandwin.com

Date: **Day #**

End of the day summary:

How many women did you chat with today?

How many women did you ask out on dates?

I reframed negative thoughts into positive thoughts: **Y/N**

Tomorrow's goals: Write your list each day

☐

☐

☐

Personal Notes & Observations:

JOURNAL

For personalized coaching: conquerandwin.com

Date: **Day #**

End of the day summary:

How many women did you chat with today?

How many women did you ask out on dates?

I reframed negative thoughts into positive thoughts: **Y/N**

Tomorrow's goals: Write your list each day

_____ ☐
_____ ☐
_____ ☐

Personal Notes & Observations:

_____
_____
_____
_____
_____
_____
_____
_____

JOURNAL

For personalized coaching: conquerandwin.com

Date: **Day #**

End of the day summary:

How many women did you chat with today?

How many women did you ask out on dates?

I reframed negative thoughts into positive thoughts: **Y/N**

Tomorrow's goals: Write your list each day

- [ ] _____
- [ ] _____
- [ ] _____

Personal Notes & Observations:

_____
_____
_____
_____
_____
_____
_____
_____

JOURNAL

For personalized coaching: conquerandwin.com

Date: **Day #**

End of the day summary:

How many women did you chat with today?

How many women did you ask out on dates?

I reframed negative thoughts into positive thoughts: **Y/N**

Tomorrow's goals: Write your list each day

☐
_____
☐
_____
☐
_____

Personal Notes & Observations:

_____
_____
_____
_____
_____
_____
_____
_____

JOURNAL

For personalized coaching: conquerandwin.com

Date: **Day #**

End of the day summary:

How many women did you chat with today?

How many women did you ask out on dates?

I reframed negative thoughts into positive thoughts: **Y/N**

Tomorrow's goals: Write your list each day

_____ ☐
_____ ☐
_____ ☐

Personal Notes & Observations:

_____
_____
_____
_____
_____
_____
_____
_____

JOURNAL

Date: **Day #**

End of the day summary:

How many women did you chat with today?

How many women did you ask out on dates?

I reframed negative thoughts into positive thoughts: **Y/N**

Tomorrow's goals: Write your list each day

_____ ☐
_____ ☐
_____ ☐

Personal Notes & Observations:

_____
_____
_____
_____
_____
_____
_____
_____

JOURNAL

For personalized coaching: conquerandwin.com

Date: **Day #**

End of the day summary:

How many women did you chat with today?

How many women did you ask out on dates?

I reframed negative thoughts into positive thoughts: **Y/N**

Tomorrow's goals: Write your list each day

- ☐
- ☐
- ☐

Personal Notes & Observations:

JOURNAL

For personalized coaching: conquerandwin.com

Date: **Day #**

End of the day summary:

How many women did you chat with today?

How many women did you ask out on dates?

I reframed negative thoughts into positive thoughts: **Y/N**

Tomorrow's goals: Write your list each day

☐

_____

_____ ☐

_____

_____ ☐

Personal Notes & Observations:

_____

_____

_____

_____

_____

_____

_____

_____

JOURNAL

For personalized coaching: conquerandwin.com

Date: **Day #**

End of the day summary:

How many women did you chat with today?

How many women did you ask out on dates?

I reframed negative thoughts into positive thoughts: **Y/N**

Tomorrow's goals: Write your list each day

- ☐
- ☐
- ☐

Personal Notes & Observations:

JOURNAL

For personalized coaching: conquerandwin.com

Date: **Day #**

End of the day summary:

How many women did you chat with today?

How many women did you ask out on dates?

I reframed negative thoughts into positive thoughts: **Y/N**

Tomorrow's goals: Write your list each day

☐

☐

☐

Personal Notes & Observations:

JOURNAL

For personalized coaching: conquerandwin.com

Date: **Day #**

End of the day summary:

How many women did you chat with today?

How many women did you ask out on dates?

I reframed negative thoughts into positive thoughts: **Y/N**

Tomorrow's goals: Write your list each day

_____ ☐
_____ ☐
_____ ☐
_____

Personal Notes & Observations:

_____
_____
_____
_____
_____
_____
_____
_____

JOURNAL

For personalized coaching: conquerandwin.com

Date: **Day #**

End of the day summary:

How many women did you chat with today?

How many women did you ask out on dates?

I reframed negative thoughts into positive thoughts: **Y/N**

Tomorrow's goals: Write your list each day

☐

_____

☐

_____

☐

_____

Personal Notes & Observations:

_____

_____

_____

_____

_____

_____

_____

_____

JOURNAL

For personalized coaching: conquerandwin.com

Date: **Day #**

End of the day summary:

How many women did you chat with today?

How many women did you ask out on dates?

I reframed negative thoughts into positive thoughts: **Y/N**

Tomorrow's goals: Write your list each day

- ☐
- ☐
- ☐

Personal Notes & Observations:

MONTHLY REVIEW:

◆ **How I rate this month overall:**

_____

_____

◆ **What did I learn this month?**

_____

_____

_____

_____

_____

My biggest accomplishment is:

_____

_____

_____

◆ **What will I Improve in the next 30 days?**

_____

_____

_____

_____

_____

JOURNAL

For personalized coaching: conquerandwin.com

Date: **Day #**

End of the day summary:

How many women did you chat with today?

How many women did you ask out on dates?

I reframed negative thoughts into positive thoughts: **Y/N**

Tomorrow's goals: Write your list each day

_____ ☐
_____ ☐
_____ ☐

Personal Notes & Observations:

_____
_____
_____
_____
_____
_____
_____

JOURNAL

For personalized coaching: conquerandwin.com

Date: **Day #**

End of the day summary:

How many women did you chat with today?

How many women did you ask out on dates?

I reframed negative thoughts into positive thoughts: **Y/N**

Tomorrow's goals: Write your list each day

- ☐
- ☐
- ☐

Personal Notes & Observations:

JOURNAL

For personalized coaching: conquerandwin.com

Date: **Day #**

End of the day summary:

How many women did you chat with today?

How many women did you ask out on dates?

I reframed negative thoughts into positive thoughts: **Y/N**

Tomorrow's goals: Write your list each day

_____ ☐
_____ ☐
_____ ☐

Personal Notes & Observations:

_____
_____
_____
_____
_____
_____
_____
_____

JOURNAL

For personalized coaching: conquerandwin.com

Date: **Day #**

End of the day summary:

How many women did you chat with today?

How many women did you ask out on dates?

I reframed negative thoughts into positive thoughts: **Y/N**

Tomorrow's goals: Write your list each day

☐
_____

☐
_____

☐
_____

Personal Notes & Observations:

_____
_____
_____
_____
_____
_____
_____
_____

JOURNAL

For personalized coaching: conquerandwin.com

Date: **Day #**

End of the day summary:

How many women did you chat with today?

How many women did you ask out on dates?

I reframed negative thoughts into positive thoughts: **Y/N**

Tomorrow's goals: Write your list each day

_____ ☐
_____ ☐
_____ ☐

Personal Notes & Observations:

_____
_____
_____
_____
_____
_____
_____
_____

JOURNAL

For personalized coaching: conquerandwin.com

Date: **Day #**

End of the day summary:

How many women did you chat with today?

How many women did you ask out on dates?

I reframed negative thoughts into positive thoughts: **Y/N**

Tomorrow's goals: Write your list each day

_____ ☐
_____ ☐
_____ ☐

Personal Notes & Observations:

_____
_____
_____
_____
_____
_____
_____
_____

JOURNAL

For personalized coaching: conquerandwin.com

Date: **Day #**

End of the day summary:

How many women did you chat with today?

How many women did you ask out on dates?

I reframed negative thoughts into positive thoughts: **Y/N**

Tomorrow's goals: Write your list each day

_____ ☐
_____ ☐
_____ ☐

Personal Notes & Observations:

_____
_____
_____
_____
_____
_____
_____
_____

JOURNAL

For personalized coaching: conquerandwin.com

Date: **Day #**

End of the day summary:

How many women did you chat with today?

How many women did you ask out on dates?

I reframed negative thoughts into positive thoughts: **Y/N**

Tomorrow's goals: Write your list each day

☐
_____

☐
_____

☐
_____

Personal Notes & Observations:

_____
_____
_____
_____
_____
_____
_____
_____

JOURNAL

For personalized coaching: conquerandwin.com

Date: **Day #**

End of the day summary:

How many women did you chat with today?

How many women did you ask out on dates?

I reframed negative thoughts into positive thoughts: **Y/N**

Tomorrow's goals: Write your list each day

_____ ☐
_____ ☐
_____ ☐
_____

Personal Notes & Observations:

_____
_____
_____
_____
_____
_____
_____
_____
_____

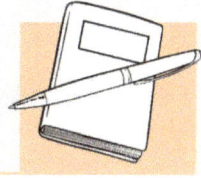

JOURNAL

For personalized coaching: conquerandwin.com

Date: **Day #**

End of the day summary:

How many women did you chat with today?

How many women did you ask out on dates?

I reframed negative thoughts into positive thoughts: **Y/N**

Tomorrow's goals: Write your list each day

_____ ☐

_____ ☐

_____ ☐

_____

Personal Notes & Observations:

_____

_____

_____

_____

_____

_____

_____

_____

JOURNAL

For personalized coaching: conquerandwin.com

Date: **Day #**

End of the day summary:

How many women did you chat with today?

How many women did you ask out on dates?

I reframed negative thoughts into positive thoughts: **Y/N**

Tomorrow's goals: Write your list each day

_____ ☐
_____ ☐
_____ ☐
_____

Personal Notes & Observations:

_____
_____
_____
_____
_____
_____
_____
_____

JOURNAL

For personalized coaching: conquerandwin.com

Date: **Day #**

End of the day summary:

How many women did you chat with today?

How many women did you ask out on dates?

I reframed negative thoughts into positive thoughts: **Y/N**

Tomorrow's goals: Write your list each day

_____ ☐
_____ ☐
_____ ☐

Personal Notes & Observations:

_____
_____
_____
_____
_____
_____
_____
_____

JOURNAL

For personalized coaching: conquerandwin.com

Date: **Day #**

End of the day summary:

How many women did you chat with today?

How many women did you ask out on dates?

I reframed negative thoughts into positive thoughts: **Y/N**

Tomorrow's goals: Write your list each day

- ☐ _____
- ☐ _____
- ☐ _____

Personal Notes & Observations:

_____
_____
_____
_____
_____
_____
_____
_____

JOURNAL

For personalized coaching: conquerandwin.com

Date: **Day #**

End of the day summary:

How many women did you chat with today?

How many women did you ask out on dates?

I reframed negative thoughts into positive thoughts: **Y/N**

Tomorrow's goals: Write your list each day

☐
_____
☐
_____
☐
_____

Personal Notes & Observations:

_____
_____
_____
_____
_____
_____
_____
_____

JOURNAL

For personalized coaching: conquerandwin.com

Date: **Day #**

End of the day summary:

How many women did you chat with today?

How many women did you ask out on dates?

I reframed negative thoughts into positive thoughts: **Y/N**

Tomorrow's goals: Write your list each day

☐
☐
☐

Personal Notes & Observations:

JOURNAL

For personalized coaching: conquerandwin.com

Date: **Day #**

End of the day summary:

How many women did you chat with today?

How many women did you ask out on dates?

I reframed negative thoughts into positive thoughts: **Y/N**

Tomorrow's goals: Write your list each day

_____ ☐
_____ ☐
_____ ☐
_____

Personal Notes & Observations:

_____
_____
_____
_____
_____
_____
_____
_____

JOURNAL

For personalized coaching: conquerandwin.com

Date: **Day #**

End of the day summary:

How many women did you chat with today?

How many women did you ask out on dates?

I reframed negative thoughts into positive thoughts: **Y/N**

Tomorrow's goals: Write your list each day

_____ ☐
_____ ☐
_____ ☐

Personal Notes & Observations:

_____
_____
_____
_____
_____
_____
_____
_____

JOURNAL

For personalized coaching: conquerandwin.com

Date: **Day #**

End of the day summary:

How many women did you chat with today?

How many women did you ask out on dates?

I reframed negative thoughts into positive thoughts: **Y/N**

Tomorrow's goals: Write your list each day

☐
_____
☐
_____
☐
_____

Personal Notes & Observations:

_____
_____
_____
_____
_____
_____
_____
_____

JOURNAL

For personalized coaching: conquerandwin.com

Date: **Day #**

End of the day summary:

How many women did you chat with today?

How many women did you ask out on dates?

I reframed negative thoughts into positive thoughts: **Y/N**

Tomorrow's goals: Write your list each day

- ☐
- ☐
- ☐

Personal Notes & Observations:

JOURNAL

For personalized coaching: conquerandwin.com

Date: **Day #**

End of the day summary:

How many women did you chat with today?

How many women did you ask out on dates?

I reframed negative thoughts into positive thoughts: **Y/N**

Tomorrow's goals: Write your list each day

- ☐ _____
- ☐ _____
- ☐ _____

Personal Notes & Observations:

_____
_____
_____
_____
_____
_____
_____
_____

JOURNAL

For personalized coaching: conquerandwin.com

Date: **Day #**

End of the day summary:

How many women did you chat with today?

How many women did you ask out on dates?

I reframed negative thoughts into positive thoughts: **Y/N**

Tomorrow's goals: Write your list each day

_____ ☐
_____ ☐
_____ ☐
_____

Personal Notes & Observations:

_____
_____
_____
_____
_____
_____
_____
_____

JOURNAL

For personalized coaching: conquerandwin.com

Date: **Day #**

End of the day summary:

How many women did you chat with today?

How many women did you ask out on dates?

I reframed negative thoughts into positive thoughts: **Y/N**

Tomorrow's goals: Write your list each day

☐

☐

☐

Personal Notes & Observations:

JOURNAL

For personalized coaching: conquerandwin.com

Date: **Day #**

End of the day summary:

How many women did you chat with today?

How many women did you ask out on dates?

I reframed negative thoughts into positive thoughts: **Y/N**

Tomorrow's goals: Write your list each day

_____ ☐
_____ ☐
_____ ☐

Personal Notes & Observations:

_____
_____
_____
_____
_____
_____
_____
_____

JOURNAL

For personalized coaching: conquerandwin.com

Date: **Day #**

End of the day summary:

How many women did you chat with today?

How many women did you ask out on dates?

I reframed negative thoughts into positive thoughts: **Y/N**

Tomorrow's goals: Write your list each day

☐

☐

☐

Personal Notes & Observations:

JOURNAL

For personalized coaching: conquerandwin.com

Date: **Day #**

End of the day summary:

How many women did you chat with today?

How many women did you ask out on dates?

I reframed negative thoughts into positive thoughts: **Y/N**

Tomorrow's goals: Write your list each day

☐
_____
☐
_____
☐
_____

Personal Notes & Observations:

_____
_____
_____
_____
_____
_____
_____
_____
_____

JOURNAL

For personalized coaching: conquerandwin.com

Date: **Day #**

End of the day summary:

How many women did you chat with today?

How many women did you ask out on dates?

I reframed negative thoughts into positive thoughts: **Y/N**

Tomorrow's goals: Write your list each day

_____ ☐
_____ ☐
_____ ☐
_____

Personal Notes & Observations:

_____
_____
_____
_____
_____
_____
_____
_____

JOURNAL

For personalized coaching: conquerandwin.com

Date: **Day #**

End of the day summary:

How many women did you chat with today?

How many women did you ask out on dates?

I reframed negative thoughts into positive thoughts: **Y/N**

Tomorrow's goals: Write your list each day

- ☐ _____
- ☐ _____
- ☐ _____

Personal Notes & Observations:

_____
_____
_____
_____
_____
_____
_____
_____

JOURNAL

For personalized coaching: conquerandwin.com

Date: **Day #**

End of the day summary:

How many women did you chat with today?

How many women did you ask out on dates?

I reframed negative thoughts into positive thoughts: **Y/N**

Tomorrow's goals: Write your list each day

- ☐
- ☐
- ☐

Personal Notes & Observations:

JOURNAL

For personalized coaching: conquerandwin.com

Date: **Day #**

End of the day summary:

How many women did you chat with today?

How many women did you ask out on dates?

I reframed negative thoughts into positive thoughts: **Y/N**

Tomorrow's goals: Write your list each day

☐

☐

☐

Personal Notes & Observations:

JOURNAL

For personalized coaching: conquerandwin.com

Date: **Day #**

End of the day summary:

How many women did you chat with today?

How many women did you ask out on dates?

I reframed negative thoughts into positive thoughts: **Y/N**

Tomorrow's goals: Write your list each day

_____ ☐
_____ ☐
_____
_____ ☐
_____

Personal Notes & Observations:

_____
_____
_____
_____
_____
_____
_____
_____

MONTHLY REVIEW:

- **How I rate this month overall:**

_____

_____

- **What did I learn this month?**

_____

_____

_____

_____

My biggest accomplishment is:

_____

_____

_____

- **What will I Improve in the next 30 days?**

_____

_____

_____

_____

.

www.ingramcontent.com/pod-product-compliance
Lightning Source LLC
Chambersburg PA
CBHW072007090426
42740CB00011B/2121